Making the Nonsense at Work
Work for You

a **Chief Energy Organizer** production

Make the Nonsense at Work Work for You

James Henry McIntosh

Make the Nonsense at Work Work for You

Published by: Chief Energy Organizer Books
                www.chiefenergyorganizer.com

Cover design by curiousant

The cartoon is based on a drawing which Ann Gadd made for one of James McIntosh's earliest talks (late 1980s) on organizational hierarchies. Ann's original drawing has been substantially modified and updated by Bronwyn McIntosh.

Printed in the United States of America
First Edition

ISBN: 978-0-6151-5247-9

This book is for
the Real Jim Wilson

When I gave Real Jim a CD with samples of
my radio recordings, he said,
"Hey, this is a book."

He was right.

And here it is.

This book is about making the nonsense at work
work for you, because...

...nonsense side-tracks you from your work,
tricks you into wrong decisions, and
trips you up short of your goals.

Nonsense stops you from
being successful.

*It will
continue to do so
until you see the sense in nonsense....*

*And learn how to make the nonsense at work
work for you.*

Contents

nonsense at work

making shift happen

The Making Of This Nonsense

Before we begin, let me explain the format and length of these snippets. These are modified versions of my twice-weekly radio broadcast on Richmond, Virginia, public radio.

When Dr Wally Johnston asked me to take over his radio show, his instructions were simple, but brutal. I had 60 seconds on air to make my point. No more. No less.

In making these recordings, I experienced a relatively unknown law of nonsense. It takes much longer to listen to a 60-second-recording than it takes to speak it. Think about that bit of nonsense for a second.

We have all been taught that people listen faster than you can speak, which is why some annoying people complete your sentences for you, often incorrectly. But that's not the case when you are told to say something meaningful within a specified time limit. Then time speeds up and you run out of time before you run out of words.

Another lesson I learned is that it takes much, much longer to write something that can be read in sixty-seconds than it takes to read it. That's another reason why I wrote the book – for those of you who want to get through these tracks even faster than the sixty seconds it will take to listen to the broadcast or the compact disc.

Now let's get on with making the nonsense at work – work for you.

nonsense at work

making shift happen

Nonsense-At-Work

The snippets of nonsense in this book will either make you think, 'Hmm, that makes sense', or 'What nonsense'. Both reactions are acceptable to me. But it would not be acceptable if you don't at least think about the sense or the nonsense.

What is nonsense? The term 'nonsense' describes absurd, ridiculous, foolish or meaningless words, ideas, or conduct. Nonsense is purely subjective: you are likely to see 'nonsense' when *you* disapprove of it. (For example, you might disapprove of the word 'bull', although others commonly use it to indicate nonsense.)

The problem with nonsense is that it side-tracks you from your work, tricks you into wrong decisions, and trips you up short of your goals. Nonsense stops you from being successful.

The bad news is that nonsense is always at work. It never stops. The good news is that there is always some sense in nonsense, if you look for it. And if you are willing to look for it, time and again you will find that you can make the nonsense at work – work for you.

Don't expect this book to help you to spot nonsense. That is simply not possible because what makes sense to me might be complete nonsense to you. Instead, the aim of this book is to help you to understand that 'nonsense' is not really nonsense. Nonsense has a purpose. In general terms, nonsense works at getting you to change your ways.

And in general terms, my purpose with this book is to help you to see the sense in nonsense so that the nonsense at work... yes, you get it.

nonsense at work

making shift happen

Nonsense At Work

In theory, an organization is a hierarchy of authority and responsibility designed to enable many individuals to work together. In reality, an organization is a hierarchy of power and rewards: the people who work there agree to strive for collective objectives, decided on within a hierarchy of power, in exchange for individual rewards based on a hierarchy of merit. The higher up you sit in the hierarchy, the greater your power and the bigger your rewards; the lower down you are, the less your power and the smaller your rewards.

In theory, the higher up you are, the better your view (perspective) and the more you can see (understand). This is why the one at the top of the hierarchy has the power to set the 'collective' objectives. On the other hand, the lower down you are, the greater your need for safety and security (because you have less power to protect yourself and smaller rewards to live on.) This is why, in practice, those at the bottom do as they are told to do.

In between the two hierarchical extremes of executive floor and factory floor, of suite and cubicle, is where nonsense is at work. In the middle are the people who want to protect the hierarchy because they dream of securing more of its power and rewards. (The people at the bottom are pressured into submission by the hierarchy and the people at the top are immune to any form of pressure – mainly because they are exerting the pressure.)

This is how the middle-people protect the hierarchy: The middle-people are charged with translating the vision from above into instructions, rules and regulations. These instructions, rules and regulations are supposedly designed to make it easier to execute the strategy. In reality, though, they do little more than to protect the hierarchy for those engaged in climbing it.

Before you say, "Nonsense!" I suggest that you study your policies and procedures more carefully.

nonsense at work

making shift happen

The No-Nonsense Way
To Read This Book

*(And a 'nonsensical' way to read your
policies and procedures.)*

The no-nonsense way to read this book is to react on the right and to think on the left. Let me explain.

Your brain has two hemispheres which are responsible for different modes of perceiving and reasoning. Words commonly used to describe left brain thinking are *logical, sequential, rational, analytical, objective, parts*. Right brain thinking is described in terms of *random, intuitive, holistic, subjective, wholes*.

Most people have a preference for one or the other of these modes. You are said to be left-brain dominant if you tend to see things in stark *either/or, black-or-white* terms. You also pride yourself at being objective, rational and logical. In other words, you know nonsense when you see it.

On the other hand, if you are right-brain dominant you tend to see things in terms of *greys* and *maybes*. You also see nothing wrong in making subjective evaluations, often based on your intuition. In other words, you are seldom sure that nonsense is really nonsense, because on the one hand it could mean one thing and on the other....

To make sense of nonsense requires you to become adept at using both modes – to become a so-called 'whole brain' thinker. You will find it easier to make the nonsense at work – work for you when you use both left and right brain modes.

This book is designed so that you can react intuitively to what you read on the right hand pages and think carefully about it on the left hand pages. Of course, you may *think* that this way is nonsense; you may even *feel* that it is nonsense. In fact, it may even annoy you to find that the questions precede the discourse (nonsense is often annoying). Read it your way, but *do* try to make shift happen – *your way*.

There are more pictures on the website showing how the African bush taught my legs to move rapidly because I had not yet learned to see properly.

Go to www.makenonsensework.com

Making Shift Happen
Left-Right, Left-Right

One lesson I learned in Africa is how to see a camouflaged animal in the bush. Here's how it's done: Look at the bush where you suspect an animal is hiding. Now shift your focus as if you are looking beyond the bush into the distance. Look through the bush as if the bush is not there. If you do this correctly, the bush will go out of focus and even 'disappear' (at least in your mind's eye). Now rock your head slowly from side to side without taking your eye off that imaginary spot in the distance. With some practice, and a bit of luck, you will become quite good at making out any form that is lurking there. (I did not need this skill to see the lioness in the picture on the previous page. Although she appears to be standing still, she was actually charging me and making an unpleasant sound. I had no need to rock my head from side to side – it was already shaking. And so were my legs.)

I never expected to find this jungle skill of any use in the city, but I do. I use it to see the sense in nonsense. Whenever I bump into what seems to me to be a well-camouflaged bit of nonsense, I stare right through it and rock my head from side to side. (Another trick I have learned is not to be put off by people staring at me and rocking *their* heads from side to side.) I call this staring and rocking 'making shift happen'. The staring and rocking creates a shift in perception that helps you to see differently (*left-brain, right-brain, left-brain, right-brain*). Seeing differently tends to change the way you respond to what you are seeing. In other words, it creates a shift in behavior.

Why do shifts matter? In today's world, things change rather fast. What you may think is sense today might very well be nonsense tomorrow. It makes little sense to get caught up in the '*what-is-now*' (the bush) and to ignore the '*what-can-be*' (the camouflaged animal). If you are stuck in the '*what-is-now*' you tend to see obstacles and limitations. On the other hand, if you anticipate the '*what-can-be*' you often see opportunities and abundance.

It takes a shift in perception to see clearly; responding appropriately takes a shift in behavior. Mostly, it takes a shift away from nonsense.

nonsense \ at work

making shift happen

Part 1

The Nonsense of Perceptions

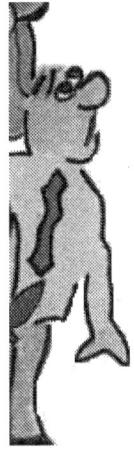

Perception is the way we process, interpret and give meaning to the information we receive via our senses. It is simply the way every *individual* makes sense of his or her world. I emphasized the word 'individual' because we all have unique ways of perceiving our world, of interpreting and making sense of it.

If we all make unique interpretations of reality, then *there are as many realities as there are people!* Intuitively, we know this cannot be, because then communication would be almost impossible. To ensure that there is at least some form of communication, we agree to share a common meaning of reality. Through these shared meanings, our different perceptions become similar (but not the same).

But we get it right most of the time. *Or do we?*

The common mistake we make is not to differentiate between what is really 'out there' (the facts) and the deduction we make from the facts. We ignore the fact that there is no reality without interpretation.

We assume that perception is objective. However, this can only be the case if we add nothing, leave nothing out, distort nothing, and misrepresent nothing in what we perceive. This is simply not possible because we constantly reconstruct and interpret reality mainly by relying on our past experiences. In other words, we *give* reality meaning. Or should I say, we give reality all the meaning it has for us.

Your perceptions might be 'wrong', they might be nonsense, but they're *yours*.

nonsense

Make shift happen

Pay attention to the expected

| Why do you think #2 makes *sense*? | What specifically about #2 do you think is *nonsense*? |

Now make your shift happen:

How can you explain
the *nonsense* you see
in #2 so that
it begins to
make *sense*
to you?

Nonsense #2

Pay attention to the expected

Did you expect me to start with Nonsense #1 instead of Nonsense #2? If so, you're probably paying attention, because something unexpected has happened. That's natural. We pay more attention when something unexpected happens.

Dealing with the unexpected is said to be the most difficult aspect of business life. My experience has taught me the opposite. The most difficult thing to manage is the expected.

Let's face it. Business is boring. It's the same nonsense over and over, day after day.

It's like driving the same car, on the same road, to the same destination at the same time every day. You must do it. And if you take your eye off what you're doing, bad things can happen.

The most successful managers I have worked with were those who had the discipline to focus on the *same* detail, over and over, day after day.

By the way, paying attention to the unexpected is one reason why sales people give more attention to new customers than to their existing ones. Doing so is not only bad for business, it's also bad manners.

nonsense

Make shift happen

Perception is reality

Why do you think #1 makes *sense*?	What specifically about #1 do you think is *nonsense*?

Now make your shift happen:

How can you explain
the *nonsense* you see
in #1 so that
it begins to
make *sense*
to you?

Here is Nonsense #1

Perception is reality

Does what you perceive 'out there' correspond with reality? You heard me name this track Nonsense #1, but in your mind it is #2. Which one is reality? Well, that depends. Two people can consider the same object, see two different things and draw different conclusions.

My silly example demonstrates how often you confront the paradox which is perception. It also shows why perceptions tend to create so many problems for anyone who is trying to understand another person's behavior – to each individual, his or her perception of reality *is* reality.

(And this is why what you see as nonsense *is* nonsense – to you.)

We happily behave as if the world around us is really as we see it, as if "seeing is believing". We would encounter far less nonsense 'out there' if we would admit to ourselves that, "I would not have seen it, if I had not already believed it to be true."

Make shift happen

Perceptual errors at work

| Why do you think #3 makes *sense*? | What specifically about #3 do you think is *nonsense*? |

Now make your shift happen:

How can you explain
the *nonsense* you see
in #3 so that
it begins to
make *sense*
to you?

Nonsense #3

Perceptual errors at work

Socially, our consensus about how to perceive and interpret reality seems to work well enough. But at work, 'well enough' is often not good enough. And yet, many managers ignore the power of perceptions and fail to manage perceptual errors.

Perceptual errors are the mistakes we make in interpreting reality and lead to ineffective responses and inappropriate behavior. What causes these errors? Mental laziness. We all do the minimum amount of mental work we think is necessary.

For example, to deal with the information overload, we use mental short-cuts and simple decision-making rules to make deductions quickly, and to draw conclusions. The problem with using mental short-cuts is that we make up our minds without considering all relevant information. No wonder we misinterpret reality!

Because we rely so much on our consensus of what constitutes reality, perceptual errors can be disastrous for team effectiveness. Your role, as a team leader or as a team member, is to keep in mind that people don't behave according to strategies and instructions. People act on their perceptions.

Please note: Perceptual errors at work create nonsense at work. Therefore, every section of this book will begin with a relevant perceptual error.

nonsense

Make shift happen

Seeing differently creates insight

Why do you think #4 makes *sense*?	What specifically about #4 do you think is *nonsense*?

Now make your shift happen:

How can you explain
the *nonsense* you see
in #4 so that
it begins to
make *sense*
to you?

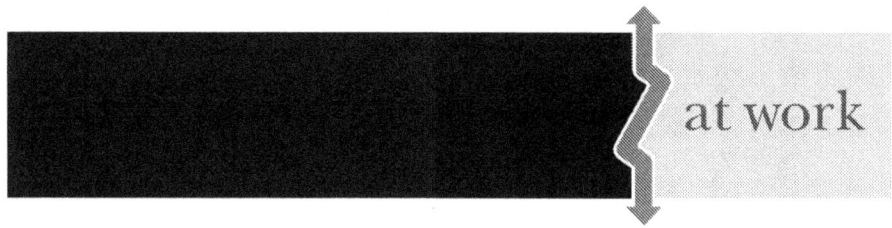

Nonsense #4

Seeing differently creates insight

Peter Drucker once wrote that selling refrigerators to the Eskimos to keep food cold is one thing. But selling refrigerators to the Eskimos to keep food from freezing is creative.

The point? Unless you see the relationship between the objects involved, (the fridge, the food, the climate and the Eskimo), you will only see the functionality of the fridge and decide that Eskimos do not need fridges. And yet, Eskimos could use something which could prevent food from freezing while keeping it fresh.

A long, long time ago two shoe-salesmen went to Africa. Soon the one wrote to his boss, "Coming home. People don't wear shoes." The other telegraphed his office, "Urgent. Send shoes. Huge untapped market."

Both were looking at the same market, but seeing it differently. Seeing differently creates insight.

nonsense

Make shift happen

Making sense... and nonsense

| Why do you think #5 makes *sense*? | What specifically about #5 do you think is *nonsense*? |

Now make your shift happen:

How can you explain
the *nonsense* you see
in #5 so that
it begins to
make *sense*
to you?

Nonsense #5

Making sense... and nonsense

Do not assume that there is complete agreement between the world around you and your perception of it. This simply cannot be because there is no reality without interpretation.

What this really means is that you imagine both the sense and the nonsense you see.

Every time you encounter nonsense, you are free to decide whether you see 'sense' or 'non-sense'. In doing so, you are the creator of sense and of nonsense. Think about that.

Deciding on what *is* nonsense and what is *not* depends on your state of mind because what matters is not nonsense itself, but how you look at it. We are taught that seeing is believing. It is more correct to say that we see what we already believe, what is already *in* us.

This is why no-one can tell with confidence what you, the individual, regard to be nonsense. And why your nonsense could quite easily be another person's sense.

nonsense at work

making shift happen

Part 2

The Nonsense of Goals

Why do you want to make the nonsense at work, work for you? Why are you studying this book? Why do you do anything? The simple answer is that you do something because you hope for a reward of some sort.

Your motive for doing something is the 'why' of human behavior. Motives spur you to action. Motives derive from your needs and desires and trigger your 'will-to-do'. Goals, on the other hand, are the 'hoped-for' rewards resulting from your actions.

In other words, you are motivated to achieve a goal because you believe that by reaching your goal you will satisfy a specific need or desire. You are 'willing-to-do' because you are 'hoping-to-get'.

Simple, isn't it? *Or is it?*

More often than not the goals we choose and set for ourselves are not very effective in maintaining our will-to-do to keep us keeping on. In other words, we set the wrong goal even though we have the right desire in mind.

And, it is in the mind where we tend to slip up. We are told to set 'realistic' goals based on a realistic consideration of the physical world 'out there'. But deciding on what is realistic and what is not depends far more on what is *in* your mind than on what is *out* there.

My point is this: The next time you are motivated to set a goal to satisfy a need, don't ignore the power of perception nor the power of projection.

nonsense

Make shift happen

Perceptual error handicaps your success

| Why do you think #6 makes *sense*? | What specifically about #6 do you think is *nonsense*? |

Now make your shift happen:

How can you explain
the *nonsense* you see
in #6 so that
it begins to
make *sense*
to you?

Nonsense #6

Perceptual error handicaps your success

Have you ever engaged in self-handicapping? Of course you have. We all do, sometimes. It's a way of protecting our self-esteem and public image.

We engage in self-handicapping when we introduce uncertainty into a situation by pointing out external factors that may, or may not, lead to poor performance or failure. Although self-handicapping cannot prevent actual failure, it can soften the blow.

We tend to use it in situations where we experience social anxiety, where the task is important such as an exam, and where we experience unexpected and unexplainable success. Of course, if the situation already has a handicap built into it, when factors that might prevent us performing well are already present, then we don't need to engage in self-handicapping.

Research shows that men tend to engage in self-handicapping more than women do. This reminds me of how Gary Player, one of the great golfers, explained his golf handicap: "The more I practice, the luckier I get."

Make shift happen

Your goal when setting goals

| Why do you think #7 makes *sense*? | What specifically about #7 do you think is *nonsense*? |

Now make your shift happen:

How can you explain
the *nonsense* you see
in #7 so that
it begins to
make *sense*
to you?

Nonsense #7

Your goal when setting goals

When setting goals, be clear and specific. Obvious, isn't it?

Maybe not, for how often have you read "safety is our goal" on the back of a big truck? No, sir, your goal is to deliver your cargo; how you do so is another matter.

And how you do so *does* matter. The more your staff members understand 'the way we do things around here', the less direct supervision they need.

'The way we do things around here' should help people *'get it'* so that they can *'get on'* with it. And in your absence, it should help them deal appropriately with unexpected nonsense.

But make sure that 'The Way' never becomes 'but we've always done it this way', for then you've stopped learning. And once you've stopped learning, safety as a goal begins to make an awful lot of sense.

Make shift happen

The 'invisible' success factors

| Why do you think #8 makes *sense*? | What specifically about #8 do you think is *nonsense*? |

Now make your shift happen:

How can you explain
the *nonsense* you see
in #8 so that
it begins to
make *sense*
to you?

Nonsense #8

The 'invisible' success factors

Normally, when we strive for success in some venture or project, we focus on those factors which impact directly and visibly on the outcome. But there are factors which are so obviously necessary that they become 'invisible' and are then ignored.

The problem is that these factors do not necessarily ensure success, but their absence guarantees failure. These factors are:

understanding, commitment, doing and *learning.*

Before you do anything, you must *understand* what is to be done, why it is to be done and how it is to be done. This understanding must make you willing to *commit* to *doing* what it takes. Finally, to ensure ongoing improvement, your doing must lead to *learning* which in turn must lead to a better understanding.

I call this the wheel of success. The wheel is common sense, which is probably why many managers don't apply it in practice.

Make shift happen

Make your resolutions stick

| Why do you think #9 makes *sense*? | What specifically about #9 do you think is *nonsense*? |

Now make your shift happen:

How can you explain
the *nonsense* you see
in #9 so that
it begins to
make *sense*
to you?

Nonsense #9

Make your resolutions stick

You've made a resolution and you've set a goal. That's the easy part. Making it stick is not. Why is that?

The first reason for the difficulty is that a resolution is a mental intention. Although you have 'thought' a resolution for the future, *you* are still stuck in the past. The trick is to move *all* of 'you' into the future.

One way of doing so is to act on the other meanings of 'resolution'. Resolution also means 'separation into components'; 'causing discord to pass into concord'; 'boldness of purpose'; and 'solving problems'.

In other words, you should understand the components that make up your resolution; remove discord that prevents commitment; be bold in execution and learn to solve problems that crop up.

The other reason resolutions don't easily stick is that resolutions tend to be about aspirations, about behaving better. Maybe a resolution to behave badly would stick more easily.

Make shift happen

Don't only build your strengths

| Why do you think #10 makes *sense*? | What specifically about #10 do you think is *nonsense*? |

Now make your shift happen:

How can you explain
the *nonsense* you see
in #10 so that
it begins to
make *sense*
to you?

Nonsense #10

Don't only build your strengths

Many populist life-skills coaches promote the idea that you should concentrate on building your strengths, while ignoring your weaknesses. They argue that you are employed and rewarded for your strengths, not to work on your weaknesses.

This is nonsense. And it is also harmful.

If you promote one or two strengths then you will be valued exactly for that and little else. Specialists are seldom credited as team players or leadership material, and they are often feared for the power their special strength gives them. In a rapidly changing world, special strengths have a nasty tendency of becoming irrelevant.

Your strengths might make you a superstar for a while in one special area, but those same strengths might make you a dysfunctional manager, parent, or spouse.

In the end, you will be valued more for being balanced and well-rounded.

nonsense at work

making shift happen

Part 3

The Nonsense of Team Work

Admit it. You achieve your goals because other people help you. How often can you honestly say, "I did this alone, on my own?" The same applies to work. Few of us do work that does not in some way involve others. Organizational work often involves working as part of a team. This is often convenient in more ways than one. It is easier to achieve goals when you have others you can count on. And it helps your self-image if you can blame others when goals are not reached.

Obviously, team work matters. But what is a team? A team exists the moment two or more people join forces to accomplish something together. However, when two or more people get together to perform a task, it becomes necessary to divide the labor and to co-ordinate the resultant activities. Doing so helps to secure the anticipated productivity benefits of synergy and economies of scale.

Quite a number of years ago Adam Smith pointed out that the reason the division of labor leads to greater productivity is because it allows people to specialize and become very good at what they do. Today we take it for granted that specialization, created by the division of labor within teams, will result in productivity gains. *Should we?*

Too often, at least for my liking, I encounter teams that allow people to specialize in nonsense, and to become very good at it too. There are two main reasons why this happens. (1) Team members forget why the team exists in the first place. (2) Members prize team cohesion above speaking out against nonsense.

When *why* the team exists begins to matter less than *that* the team exists, you have a team which has become very good at.... But I'm sure you can figure that out for yourself.

Make shift happen

Perceptual error of balanced teams

| Why do you think #11 makes *sense*? | What specifically about #11 do you think is *nonsense*? |

Now make your shift happen:

How can you explain
the *nonsense* you see
in #11 so that
it begins to
make *sense*
to you?

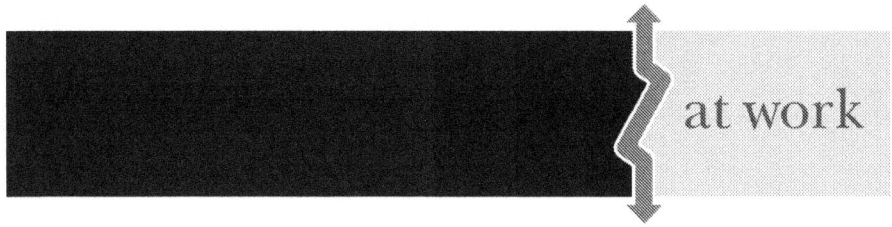

Nonsense #11

Perceptual error of balanced teams

Balance in a team makes for a pleasant team experience. However, balance can make a team less effective because effectiveness depends on exploring differing ideas.

Balance exists when people like each other and express similar views. Imbalance results when they like each other and *disagree*. Not being in balance is an unpleasant state and team members will want to restore balance.

How? Well, one person can convince the others to change their views. Or they could decide to dislike each other instead. Once they dislike each other, they become relatively indifferent as to whether they agree or disagree.

Why do we do this? We tend to like people who express similar attitudes and judgements to ours because they provide 'evidence' that we are correct. It feels nice to be correct. Obviously, if someone disagrees with us, it has the opposite effect.

The leadership trick is to get your people to disagree without becoming disagreeable.

Make shift happen

Team work down the river

| Why do you think #12 makes *sense*? | What specifically about #12 do you think is *nonsense*? |

Now make your shift happen:

How can you explain
the *nonsense* you see
in #12 so that
it begins to
make *sense*
to you?

Nonsense #12

Team work down the river

Team building exercises make me nervous. At best, they teach people how to do meaningless things together; at worst, they produce the opposite effect.

This happens when the focus is on team building instead of on a work-related outcome. You don't want people who are good at liking one another and trusting one another and paddling well together. You need people who care so much about the outcome that they overcome their liking to deal with any member who is not delivering.

A friend was once told to build better team work between her staff and her client by going river rafting. In her own words: "Before we went on the river, I thought he was an idiot. But now I know he's an idiot."

So much for team building. What should have mattered was the work they produced together, not whether they could paddle together.

Make shift happen

Do you really want team work?

Why do you think #13 makes *sense*?	What specifically about #13 do you think is *nonsense*?

Now make your shift happen:

How can you explain
the *nonsense* you see
in #13 so that
it begins to
make *sense*
to you?

Nonsense #13

Do you really want team work?

Often, the most visible result of poor team work is inefficiency, whether in the form of wasted resources, wasted time, or wasted effort. No wonder managers normally tackle team problems from an efficiency perspective and immediately set out to improve team work.

Yet, the fact that it seems necessary to teach people how to work together should warn you that you are confusing symptoms and causes.

An efficiency perspective aims to fix what is perceived to be wrong and automatically draws your attention to symptoms. On the other hand, an effectiveness perspective aims to achieve desired results and outcomes; hence this approach tends to make you focus on underlying causes.

Note that an effectiveness perspective does not concern itself with team work because team work is not really the desired outcome. What is desired is the output that the team should produce.

Make shift happen

Poor team work by design

| Why do you think #14 makes *sense*? | What specifically about #14 do you think is *nonsense*? |

Now make your shift happen:

How can you explain
the *nonsense* you see
in #14 so that
it begins to
make *sense*
to you?

Nonsense #14

Poor team work by design

Today, many people acknowledge Edwards Deming as the father of total quality management. Yet, when he first shared his ideas, American managers chose to ignore him. At the time, one would not use the words quality and Japanese in the same sentence. This could be why Deming found a very receptive audience in Japan for his quality ideas.

We all know what happened next.

Why did American managers find his ideas unacceptable? Deming maintained that people do not set out to produce poor quality. Instead, the systems and procedures, designed by managers, prevent people from delivering quality.

The same argument applies to team work: People don't set out to work poorly together. Poor team work is often the result of inappropriate systems, procedures, management style or organizational culture. So, to improve quality and team work, get rid of the nonsense.

Make shift happen

From co-operation to sub-optimization

| Why do you think #15 makes *sense*? | What specifically about #15 do you think is *nonsense*? |

Now make your shift happen:

How can you explain
the *nonsense* you see
in #15 so that
it begins to
make *sense*
to you?

Nonsense #15

From co-operation to sub-optimization

Quite correctly, managers want people to co-operate. But be warned: co-operation can lead to sub-optimization.

Whenever people try to co-operate, there is a risk that everyone will ultimately perform at the level of the lowest contributor or the weakest member. This happens because:

1 co-operation does not necessarily happen amongst equals;
2 the weakest member cannot hide and is aware of being weak; and
3 nobody likes feeling that they are doing more than others without receiving more in return.

This can create a pathological state where the weak want to be 'rescued' and the strong wonder why they should bother. The weak sense this, and create 'irritations' (mainly through passive-aggressive behavior) so that the strong are kept off-balance. In this way, the weak claim some power.

The outcome? Although co-operation is meant to make all parties perform better, it more often leads to sub-optimization.

nonsense ⟩ at work

making shift happen

Part 4

The Nonsense of Organizations

What is an organization? In many ways it is simply a big team made up of multiple sub-teams. Keep in mind what I said about teams in the previous section. People work together in teams because they believe that many people can achieve more than one person can on his own. However, as soon as you have many people involved in doing something to achieve a common goal, then the activities of these people must be co-ordinated.

In an informal group of friends, this co-ordination is achieved through informal agreement known as mutual adjustment. Mutual adjustment does not work very well in organizations. The main reason for this is that people in organizations don't really share a common purpose. Instead, they agree to strive for collective objectives, decided within a hierarchy of power, in exchange for individual rewards based on a hierarchy of merit. Nevertheless, as a means of channeling the collective energies of disparate individuals, the organization serves society quite well. *Or does it?*

Not only do we give the organization a legal status. We also give it 'life' by assuming that it exists independently of the people who energize it. The outcome is that we, on the outside, are too quick to blame any nonsense on the organization instead of on the people who are the organization. And the people on the inside are too quick to blame any nonsense at work on policies and procedures, on bureaucracy and red-tape, instead of on themselves, those who perpetuate the flawed designs. We blame the organization when we should be blaming the individuals who comprise the organization.

Because our rewards are individual and our objectives are collective, we find it easy to hide behind the 'collective' and ignore that we are individually responsible. As long as we share the collective cloak to hide our individual complicity, we share the blame.

Make shift happen

Perceptual error attributes behavior

Why do you think #16 makes *sense*?

What specifically about #16 do you think is *nonsense*?

Now make your shift happen:

How can you explain
the *nonsense* you see
in #16 so that
it begins to
make *sense*
to you?

Nonsense #16

Perceptual error attributes behavior

A challenge we all face in organizations is how to interpret the behavior of the many people around us. Behavior can be caused by an almost infinite number of factors. But because we are mentally lazy, we tend to focus on only two: whether the behavior stemmed from internal factors or external causes.

This mental laziness triggers another perceptual error, namely the fundamental attribution error. We tend to explain other people's behavior in terms of internal (or dispositional) causes rather than in terms of external (or situational) causes.

For example, when you see someone trip you are more likely to perceive that person as clumsy rather than to assume that she tripped over some physical object. Yet, if *you* tripped in the street, you would blame it on an external cause, not on being clumsy.

We do this because we take the easy way. We focus on people's overt actions, while treating the context in which the action takes place as less important.

This is why you might think that there is nothing wrong with accusing someone of being a bureaucrat, while blaming your own obstructionist behavior on organizational red-tape.

Make shift happen

Organizations are strange concoctions

| Why do you think #17 makes *sense*? | What specifically about #17 do you think is *nonsense*? |

Now make your shift happen:

How can you explain
the *nonsense* you see
in #17 so that
it begins to
make *sense*
to you?

Nonsense #17

Organizations are strange concoctions

Organizations are staffed with people who agree to strive for collective objectives in exchange for individual rewards. These people agree on a code of conduct and also to follow instructions.

Those who don't accept the purpose as mutual, the codes as worthy, or the instructions as valid, are kicked out.

At best, it becomes a place where those who *do* think differently, learn to conform. At worst, it becomes staffed with like-minded people inclined towards pre-judgement and prejudice.

We have created a place where the person who critically assesses ideas is labeled an obstructionist; where the one who speaks the truth is undiplomatic; where the expert hired for her knowledge is told that "we've always done it this way" and where the one who agrees with us and tells us what we like to hear is promoted.

What hilarious nonsense!

Make shift happen

The Trojan Horse in your organization

Why do you think #18
makes *sense*?

What specifically about #18
do you think is *nonsense*?

Now make your shift happen:

How can you explain
the *nonsense* you see
in #18 so that
it begins to
make *sense*
to you?

Nonsense #18

The Trojan Horse in your organization

Most people know the Greek legend of the Trojan horse, but not many people know that at least one senior person in the hierarchy of Troy was suspicious of *that* horse. We know that he was ignored.

Consider a Trojan horse incident in your own organization. With hindsight it should be clear that one of the following situations existed at the time:

1) No-one spotted the threat.
2) Someone did suspect something, but kept quiet.
3) Someone did suspect and did speak out, but was not heard.
4) Someone did suspect and was heard, but was ignored.

No organization or team can be effective if any of the above four points apply to it. Obviously, it is difficult to do anything if no-one spotted the threat. But it is always within your power to listen to others. If you don't, then be ready to welcome another Trojan horse.

Make shift happen

Business is simple

Why do you think #19 makes *sense*?	What specifically about #19 do you think is *nonsense*?

Now make your shift happen:

How can you explain
the *nonsense* you see
in #19 so that
it begins to
make *sense*
to you?

Nonsense #19

Business is simple

I once read about a meeting of a well-known manufacturer of ovens. The CEO sat listening to the discussion about quality problems with the latest model. Sales people reported about unhappy customers; quality control people defended the production team by quoting statistics.

Finally, the CEO lost patience and asked, "Are you saying that we are selling ovens that don't work? Well, get the hell out of here and fix them!"

Indeed, business is that simple.

I am cynical enough to suspect that the over supply of business schools, the worship of the latest management fad, and the rapid adoption of business buzz words all merely serve to give management an aura of complexity.

I think this stems from a subconscious yearning for business to appear difficult enough to warrant CEOs earning more than scientists, healthcare professionals, teachers... in fact, more than anyone else.

nonsense

Make shift happen

Why organizations (and teams) struggle and fail

Why do you think #20 makes *sense*?	What specifically about #20 do you think is *nonsense*?

Now make your shift happen:

How can you explain
the *nonsense* you see
in #20 so that
it begins to
make *sense*
to you?

Nonsense #20

Why organizations (and teams) struggle and fail

Remember 14 August 2003? On that day about 50 million people in the US and Canada had no electricity. The official task force blamed the blackout on overgrown trees which the power utility's linesmen had not pruned away from the power lines.

But was that the cause or a nonsense symptom?

Managers are taught to think in terms of productivity and efficiency. The more you produce with less, the higher your productivity and your efficiency. However, no electricity does not really show zero productivity. It simply highlights the huge contribution energy utilities make to our quality of life.

I wonder what the linesmen would have done about the trees if they were taught to think in terms of contribution instead of productivity and efficiency.

That is why I say organizations struggle and fail when they focus on productivity and efficiency at the expense of contribution and effectiveness.

nonsense } at work

making shıft happen

Part 5

The Nonsense of Leadership

In *Nonsense #20* I suggested that organizations struggle and fail when they focus on productivity and efficiency at the expense of contribution and effectiveness. In the organization, who decides on what the focus should be? Yes, that's right. The person at the top. The one we call "our leader" or "dear leader". Even though, in most cases, this person is not dear to us and often lacks basic leadership skills.

So what is leadership? I once got into trouble for offering the following definition at a corporate leadership development retreat: *Leadership is the art of getting others to do what you have been putting off doing for weeks.* I have mellowed over the years and now explain leadership as follows: *Leadership is about convincing; management is about controlling.* Clear and simple, isn't it? *Or is it?*

The problem, of course, is that most organizations are designed with control in mind. Managers find it far easier to use the power of the hierarchy to subdue and exploit than to use leadership skills to convince and inspire. (This is one reason why it is easier for organizations to focus on efficiency and not on effectiveness.)

Think of it this way. Leaders convince and inspire the multiple subgroups (that make up the organization) to *achieve* together. Managers control and manipulate the various groups into *working* together.

Hold on a minute. Before you think that leadership, with its ability to convince and inspire, is the answer to organizational nonsense, heed Peter Drucker. He warned that one should not admire 'leadership' per se. This is what he said: "The three greatest leaders of the 20th century were Hitler, Stalin, and Mao. If that's leadership, I want no part of it."

Make shift happen

Perceptual error creates false consensus

| Why do you think #21 makes *sense*? | What specifically about #21 do you think is *nonsense*? |

Now make your shift happen:

How can you explain
the *nonsense* you see
in #21 so that
it begins to
make *sense*
to you?

Nonsense #21

Perceptual error creates false consensus

Why is it important for team leaders to understand and manage perceptual errors? – because perceptual errors result in us interpreting reality incorrectly. This leads to ineffective responses and inappropriate behavior, which in turn reduce team effectiveness.

A perceptual error which leaders, in particular, should watch out for is the false consensus effect. We tend to assume that others behave or think like we do to a greater extent than is actually the case. For example, smokers tend to believe that a greater number of people smoke than the actual number who do smoke.

Why do we do this? Firstly, we like to think that others agree with us, because this means that we are "right". Secondly, due to a general lack of diversity in the work-place, we tend to work with people who already share our views.

You can counter the false consensus effect by simply having people around who think differently. Oh yes, and allowing them to speak out.

Make shift happen

Don't waste my time

| Why do you think #22 makes *sense*? | What specifically about #22 do you think is *nonsense*? |

Now make your shift happen:

How can you explain
the *nonsense* you see
in #22 so that
it begins to
make *sense*
to you?

Nonsense #22

Don't waste my time

In writing this book, I am not restricted by the radio broadcaster's schedule, so why do I stick to the word-length discipline that translates to sixty-seconds on air? Because I don't want to waste your time.

Let me make a prediction: The age has come when people will judge their time spent at work as *time wasted* or *time not wasted*. And they will blame their so-called leaders if they feel their time was wasted.

I have seen people *so* angry, when they thought their time had been wasted, that not even financial rewards could sweeten the bitterness with which they remembered those whom they held responsible for a loss they could never recover.

Your time is limited. This is why I say that true leaders don't waste your time.

So, dear leader, how *do* you not waste our time? Make your intentions clear. That way followers can decide whether or not they want to be part of the outcome you have in mind – whether they want to invest their time with *you*.

nonsense

Make shift happen

Leaders choose words carefully

| Why do you think #23 makes *sense*? | What specifically about #23 do you think is *nonsense*? |

Now make your shift happen:

How can you explain
the *nonsense* you see
in #23 so that
it begins to
make *sense*
to you?

Nonsense #23

Leaders choose words carefully

Let me remind you: Leaders who make their intentions clear don't waste their followers' time. I admit that there is a small problem with this statement. Let me explain.

A leader can never not lead. You lead by what you do *and* you lead by what you don't do. That is what it really means to lead by example, whether the example is 'good' or 'bad'. But we cannot lead with intentions because intentions are not 'visible' examples – until acted out, they are unfulfilled promises. Words are the next best thing for expressing our intentions.

However, words can be ambiguous, assuming a different meaning in the mind of the listener. For example, what does 'bi-monthly' mean? 'Twice every month' or 'every second month'?

Wise leaders are deliberate in their use of language. They choose words carefully, selecting specific words for the exact meaning they wish to communicate.

The problem is that we have allowed slang, jargon, and our innate human laziness to shrink our vocabulary. The gap of misunderstanding is increasing between what the wise are saying and what we are hearing. And as we become tone-deaf, intentions remain unfulfilled.

nonsense

Make shift happen

'I don't know'

Why do you think #24 makes *sense*?	What specifically about #24 do you think is *nonsense*?

Now make your shift happen:

How can you explain
the *nonsense* you see
in #24 so that
it begins to
make *sense*
to you?

Nonsense #24

'I don't know'

I want to share with you the three most important words I have learned as a consultant. They are "I don't know".

Yes, I know that consultants are not normally paid for not knowing. Nor are leaders. But leaders and consultants can be at their most effective when they admit to not knowing.

When a leader makes a statement, outlines a plan, or offers a solution, followers stop thinking. On the other hand, when someone who is supposed to know admits to not knowing, it creates a space for others to fill with different perspectives and new ideas.

It is a wise leader who, even when knowing, occasionally says, "I don't know". Try it; you might even learn something from your followers.

I have learned from my clients and got paid for it.

Make shift happen

Abuse of power leads to group-think

| Why do you think #25 makes *sense?* | What specifically about #25 do you think is *nonsense?* |

Now make your shift happen:

How can you explain
the *nonsense* you see
in #25 so that
it begins to
make *sense*
to you?

Nonsense #25

Abuse of power leads to group-think

Don't forget to exercise your power. If you don't use it, no one will know that you have it. But take care how you use it or you might abuse it.

One serious outcome of the abuse of power is group-think. Group-think is the tendency of group members to take decisions uncritically and without due thought, particularly when the decisions are recommended by powerful members of the group.

You have group-think when your colleagues think they simply cannot fail; when they assume that they are of one mind; when they believe that the group's decisions are morally justified; when they put pressure on dissenters; when they practice self-censorship or when they stereotype other groups as weak, ineffective, or stupid.

Group-think is often fear-based because no one in the group is willing to speak up and against. So watch how you use your power or watch how poor decisions multiply in your group.

nonsense at work

making shift happen

Part 6

The Nonsense of Culture

Leaders lead by example, by doing. You lead by what you do and you lead by what you don't do. You can never not lead. That is why leaders have such a great impact on the culture of an organization.

The word 'culture' means the particular form, stage, or type of intellectual development of a civilization. It also means production, as in fish culture, or bee culture. This is why it is so useful to refer to a corporate culture. The term 'corporate culture' relates both to the 'form, stage, or type of development' of an organization, as well as to how that development contributes, or does not, to a desired outcome such as efficient production or customer service.

Corporate culture is the 'mechanism' through which the corporate strategy is implemented. If there is a poor match between the what-must-be-done (strategy) and the how-we-do-things-here (culture), then the strategy will be poorly executed. This is why it matters that you have a good, strong culture. *Or does it?*

Labeling a culture as 'good' or 'bad' is counter-productive. 'Good' or 'bad' are value judgements which inhibit the search for solutions or betterment. Instead, labeling a culture as 'effective' or 'ineffective' begs the question: 'What is the purpose of our culture?' This question is likely to trigger a search for how to change the way-we-do-things-here to make the organization more effective.

Understanding a culture in terms of effectiveness will also guard against the dangers of sameness. Too often a culture achieves nothing more than to attract like-minded individuals who see the world from the same perspective. Like-minded people make for pleasant companions, but they tend to make the same mistakes.

nonsense

Make shift happen

Perceptual error shares your feeling

Why do you think #26 makes *sense*?	What specifically about #26 do you think is *nonsense*?

Now make your shift happen:

How can you explain
the *nonsense* you see
in #26 so that
it begins to
make *sense*
to you?

Nonsense #26

Perceptual error shares your feelings

People tend either to keep quiet about bad news or to distort it to make it more palatable. We do so because we realize that bad news results in bad feelings and so we will be liked less if we pass it on.

It seems obvious enough that people like anyone who makes them feel good and dislike anyone who makes them feel bad. Less obvious is the fact that we also tend to react to those people with whom we associate the feelings we feel at the time.

For instance, if you receive good news, the chances are that you will like the person who merely happened to be with you at the time, even though he or she was not responsible for the good news in the first place.

Why do we do this? It seems that we associate people around us with our emotional state and evaluate and treat them accordingly. So, don't let your bad mood determine how you treat your colleagues, especially if they did not cause your bad mood in the first place. If you do, you'll become the bad news.

Make shift happen

The way we do things here

| Why do you think #27 makes *sense*? | What specifically about #27 do you think is *nonsense*? |

Now make your shift happen:

How can you explain
the *nonsense* you see
in #27 so that
it begins to
make *sense*
to you?

Nonsense #27

The way we do things here

Why does organizational culture matter? Consider this: As a manager you cannot imagine all the things that could possibly go wrong and then dictate the appropriate response an employee should make. Some form of social influence is needed to guide attitudes and behaviors.

We use three types of social influence, namely obedience, compliance and conformity. Obedience is obvious. Compliance happens when others adhere to a standard or regulation that you have requested. Conformity happens when individuals change behavior and attitudes in order to adhere to the generally accepted rules or views on how they should behave.

Conformity is the basic purpose of a culture, to make it obvious that this is *the way we do things here*. In other words, culture is the mechanism through which your strategy is implemented.

But be warned – it is extremely difficult, if not impossible, to change a culture. You should either work with what you've got or change your strategy.

Make shift happen

Good culture gone bad

Why do you think #28 makes *sense*?	What specifically about #28 do you think is *nonsense*?

Now make your shift happen:

How can you explain
the *nonsense* you see
in #28 so that
it begins to
make *sense*
to you?

Nonsense #28

Good culture gone bad

Would you say that your organization has a 'good' or a 'bad' culture? Don't bother. It makes no sense to evaluate a culture as either 'good' or 'bad'. What matters is whether it is effective at producing the outcome you want.

Organizational culture is effective if employees can do their work without worrying about the support of colleagues. This is called horizontal effectiveness. You have it when different individuals can blindly co-ordinate their activities and save on communication costs.

Vertical effectiveness happens when followers can guess what to do without having to wait for instructions. When this happens, you save on the costs associated with delegating and monitoring.

Always remember that culture is simply *the way we do things here*. If you are not clear about the outcome you want, then *the way you do things here* might result in bad things happening around here instead.

nonsense

Make shift happen

When culture becomes dangerous

| Why do you think #29 makes *sense*? | What specifically about #29 do you think is *nonsense*? |

Now make your shift happen:

How can you explain
the *nonsense* you see
in #29 so that
it begins to
make *sense*
to you?

Nonsense #29

When culture becomes dangerous

I have often stressed the importance of organizational culture, so let me for once argue against culture.

Your culture is meant to smooth the way things are done by defining what is acceptable and 'normal'. However, because your culture aims to stamp out the unacceptable and the 'abnormal', it can force conformity in thinking and behavior.

Therein lies the danger: your culture can inhibit creativity, innovation, and change.

Note that unacceptable or abnormal behavior can be perceived as 'normal' in a different context. This is so because 'abnormal' behavior is defined as such by those in a group who are powerful enough to make the definition stick.

History shows how often abnormal behavior has triggered beneficial change. Therapists and coaches therefore run the risk of delaying or inhibiting social change and paradigm shifts by trying to cure abnormal behavior.

Make shift happen

We, the enemy within

Why do you think #30 makes *sense*?	What specifically about #30 do you think is *nonsense*?

Now make your shift happen:

How can you explain
the *nonsense* you see
in #30 so that
it begins to
make *sense*
to you?

Nonsense #30

We, the enemy within

We know that success comes from listening and paying attention to customers. And we know that paying attention to what our competitors are doing can uncover potential opportunities and threats.

For the same reasons, we also know that we should pay attention to the people inside our organization. But we don't, not really. Most of the attention we pay them is in the form of instructions, rules, and regulations.

To get things done right, we rely more and more on policies and procedures instead of on our culture and values, on the way we do things here. No wonder we spend so much time and energy neutralizing internal forces while almost ignoring customers and competitors.

When we fail to see our repetitive internal struggles as odd behavior, we have become what Carl Jung called the enemy within. And we remain the enemy within as long as we deny that *we* create our obstacles to success.

nonsense } at work

making shıft happen

Part 7

The Nonsense of Being a Worker

Consider the following statements: Leaders lead by example. Culture is defined as *'the-way-we-do-things-here'*. Therefore, a matching leadership definition would be *'do-as-I-do'*. This definition may apply at certain levels of the hierarchy, but not at the lowest. Even though management has evolved in theory, in practice most workers still experience a completely different culture. This culture can be defined as *'do-as-you-are-told'*.

Why is this? In our organizations, there is a clear separation between those who manage and those who do the work; between those who decide and instruct and those who are expected to listen and to obey. In cruder terms, the separation is between those who are paid to think and those who are paid to do as they are told.

This treatment of workers is largely the result of the nature of the work that workers do. Unless specific skills are required, a worker is not perceived as unique, but as being interchangeable with any other worker. It is this thinking which has resulted in a worker being perceived as a cost to the organization and not as an asset. And we all know that a cost is a 'bad' thing which must be minimized. Nevertheless, this brutal focus on *'do-as-we-are-told-to-do'* continues to deliver the superior results demanded by a competitive capitalist environment. *Or does it?*

In reality, managers do not want the whole worker present, only those parts of him required to produce the desired output. Even our language promotes this attitude: we speak of a 'hired-hand', not a 'hired-man'. This explains why few managers care about worker motivation as a means of increasing worker productivity. Being a mere disposable commodity, a worker's motivation is never a management issue. The worker either does as he or she is told to do, or is told to leave. In today's rapidly changing business environment, the catch is becoming obvious: This approach only works as long as you don't run out of workers – or as long as the nature of work itself does not change.

nonsense

Make shift happen

Perceptual error keeps you mum

| Why do you think #31 makes *sense*? | What specifically about #31 do you think is *nonsense*? |

Now make your shift happen:

How can you explain
the *nonsense* you see
in #31 so that
it begins to
make *sense*
to you?

Nonsense #31

Perceptual error keeps you mum

The kings of old showed how those in power react to bad news: the bearer lost his head. The difference today is that the one most likely to lose his head is the worker. And the similarity? The boss at the top makes decisions of great import based on a steady stream of *good* news.

Yes, the boss decides on salary increases, bonuses, promotions, and so on. But this does not explain why we assume that bearing bad news will be bad for us personally.

Actually, this is a very common problem: people just don't like being the bearers of bad news. Social psychologists call this the MUM effect. People tend to either keep quiet about bad news or distort it to make it more palatable.

Research has uncovered why we do this: We do this not because we feel personal discomfort about sharing bad news or because we feel sorry for the recipient. We do so because we realize that bad news results in bad feelings. And we know intuitively that these bad feelings could translate into us being liked less, simply for passing on the bad news.

Make shift happen

Workers save the organization

| Why do you think #32 makes *sense*? | What specifically about #32 do you think is *nonsense*? |

Now make your shift happen:

How can you explain
the *nonsense* you see
in #32 so that
it begins to
make *sense*
to you?

Nonsense #32

Workers save the organization

Today, the term 'worker' has little to do with manual or industrial-type work. It has more to do with the way managers perceive and treat the people who are at the lowest output producing level of the organization.

At this basic level, workers are mere commodities because they are plentiful, cheap, inter-changeable and disposable. When there is more work to be done, more workers are hired; when there is less work to be done, workers are discarded until the number of workers more closely matches the amount of work to be done.

This insidious practice stems from the industrial revolution when, for the first time, large groups of workers were paid by the hour. And to this day, workers carry the cost of 'saving' the organization from financial ruin.

No wonder debates on the minimum hourly rate for workers still raise tempers on both sides of the divide.

Make shift happen

Pay-for-output, reward-for-input

| Why do you think #33 makes *sense*? | What specifically about #33 do you think is *nonsense*? |

Now make your shift happen:

How can you explain
the *nonsense* you see
in #33 so that
it begins to
make *sense*
to you?

Nonsense #33

Pay-for-output, reward-for-input

Much of modern management stems from Frederick Taylor's Scientific Management methodology, formally introduced in 1911, almost one hundred years ago.

One legacy of Taylor's thinking is the idea that workers should be paid for how much they produce in a given time period, and not for the number of hours they actually worked. In other words, pay-for-output and not for time put in.

However, a great deal of what a manager does is intangible, without immediate outputs or results. From a worker's perspective, it can appear as if managers are rewarded for merely being at work, for the time they put in. This payment for output-by-workers versus reward for input-by-managers is often at the root of workers feeling that they are being exploited.

This already big gap between pay-for-output and reward-for-input continues to increase as we shift from brawn-power to brain-power. And workers' discontent increases along with it.

nonsense

Make shift happen

Cherish your unreasonable people

| Why do you think #34 makes *sense*? | What specifically about #34 do you think is *nonsense*? |

Now make your shift happen:

How can you explain
the *nonsense* you see
in #34 so that
it begins to
make *sense*
to you?

Nonsense #34

Cherish your unreasonable people

George Bernard Shaw once wrote that, "The reasonable man adapts himself to the world. The unreasonable one persists in trying to adapt the world to himself. Therefore all progress depends on the unreasonable man."

How do you react to the unreasonable people in your organization? Do you heed them and engage with them? Do you sanction and discipline them? Or do you ignore them and hope that they will go away?

A prime role of a leader is to evaluate, influence and direct the behavior of others. In doing so, the leader defines the context within which behavior will be perceived as either reasonable or unreasonable.

But deciding on what is reasonable and what is not depends far more on what is in your mind than on the state of mind of the person whom you are observing.

What am I trying to tell you? Your perception of what is reasonable, and your response to unreasonableness could determine your organization's rate of progress.

Make shift happen

When capable employees leave

| Why do you think #35 makes *sense*? | What specifically about #35 do you think is *nonsense*? |

Now make your shift happen:

How can you explain
the *nonsense* you see
in #35 so that
it begins to
make *sense*
to you?

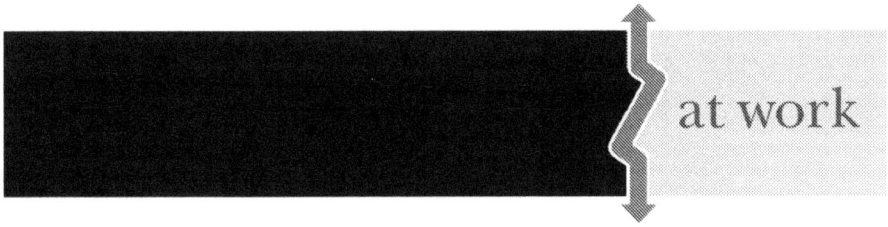

Nonsense #35

When capable employees leave

Let's explore one of those vicious cycles so often found in organizations.

To function at an acceptable level, inept individuals require rules and regulations. But capable individuals tend to feel stifled in an environment where they are constantly told what to do and how to do it. And so they leave.

As the balance in the work force swings to more inept workers and fewer capable ones, mistakes and inefficiencies increase. This serves to confirm management's suspicion that workers are either incompetent or subversive. Managers now respond by tightening their hold over the workers, forcing the last of the capable ones to run for the exits.

Now for the kicker: Because incompetent workers are less likely to confront managers, the latter end up believing that those who stay prefer a highly regimented environment.

nonsense at work
making shift happen

the end of nonsense

welcome to our side

Standing
at the nonsense divide

If you have read all the way through and answered the questions, then you and I probably now agree on this one point: Although no-one can tell with confidence what you regard to be nonsense, we can say with confidence that 'nonsense' is anything that stops you from being successful. The moment you realize that, you will find yourself at the nonsense divide.

The what?   The nonsense divide.

The nonsense divide is that imaginary line, that hyphen, which separates 'non' and 'sense' so that we find sense on the one side and 'no sense' on the other. It is the gap between the wheat and the chaff, between success and not-quite-success.

It is that mind-spirit space which separates 'any thing' from the 'right thing'. It is the mental gap between doing something and doing the right thing. It is the spiritual disconnect between merely having a job and working with purpose and meaning.

You can arrive at the divide due to some crisis in your organization, your job, or even in your life. That does happen. But more often, the divide opens out of the mundane, slowly and quietly, as everyday nonsense erodes your chances for success.

Undoubtedly, you have already crossed many nonsense divides. Merely being alive creates situations where an understanding you thought was clear, or a belief you held dear, clashes with your direct experience. Every clash opens a new divide.

Whether through a crisis or a buildup of the mundane, sooner or later you will arrive at another nonsense divide. Standing at the edge of the divide, you must decide which side is sense, and which is non-sense.

Welcome to our side

nonsense at work

making shift happen

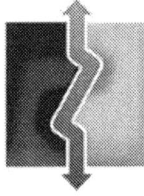

The people who helped this book directly
(Many others helped unknowingly)

The trigger Dr Wallace Johnston (Dr Wally): When he asked me to substitute for him on the radio, he inadvertently triggered the creation of the radio MP3 files which led to this book and the CD. Dr Wally was a professor in business management at Virginia Commonwealth University before he became a columnist, commentator and speaker. (Find out more on www.askdrwally.com. And read why he wanted to be the Lone Ranger on www.nonsensedivide.com.)

The pusher James Wilson III (The Real Jim Wilson): Real Jim gently prodded and asked nonsense questions. Finally, seeming to lose patience, he pushed (read more on www.nonsensedivide.com). Oh yes, he introduced me to Dr Wally.

The editor Julie Hattingh: Julie is more than merely my editor. She is also the lady of the hug. The poem I wrote about her tells it all - read it on www.nonsensedivide.com

The facilitator Elizabeth Roark: With care, patience, and an ever-present smile, Elizabeth provides the organizational home and infrastructure I need to work in.

The muse Bronwyn, my wife, lover, budget director, yoga teacher, cook, friend and mother of my children.

Thank you all

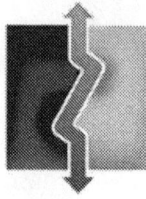

More stuff on nonsense

You will find lots more nonsense on our web sites:

www.NonsenseAtWork.com

www.NonsenseDivide.com

For example, you can subscribe to the e-newsletter about nonsense at work and find free articles, papers, sound-files (from the radio show), stories written by readers telling of their own 'crossing the nonsense divide', and so on. You will also find out where to buy our books, CDs and DVDs.

Lastly, you will find updates and previews on the latest books currently being written, CDs being recorded and DVDs being produced. As I said, nonsense never stops.

CROSSING THE NONSENSE DIVIDE
Steps to finding *your* path to a successful life

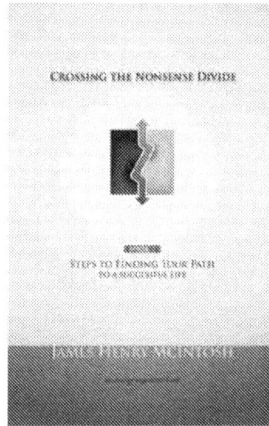

Crossing the Nonsense Divide is a personal journey about making choices. It's about choosing to create a successful life that, in the end, makes sense to you. Most of us are prevented from living successful lives by 'nonsense'. But what is 'nonsense'? 'Nonsense' describes absurd, ridiculous, foolish or meaningless words, ideas, or conduct. It is purely subjective: you are likely to see 'nonsense' when *you* disapprove of it. For example, you might 'see' the following statement as nonsense:

It does not matter whether you understand your life; it matters that you live it.

Actually, that is almost a bit of nonsense.... What really matters is that you *choose* to live it. Your freedom to choose makes you a creator and even deciding not to choose is an act of creation. That's right, you are creating your life *even when you are choosing to live with nonsense.*

"I found his writing to be very thought-provoking, often requiring me put down his book to digest some of his ideas and consider how they actually apply to my life." *Al Covington - Project Manager*

"Few books pack so much wisdom and guidance into such a succinct tome. Crossing the Nonsense Divide is dense with insight." *Julie Joyce - HR Consultant*

"I have seen how this no nonsense approach has changed lives and how it has helped those who have changed, to unwittingly help others. It is never too late to begin from where you are. Read it!" *Ray Hattingh Management & IT Consultant*

"If we could discard our collection of nonsense, and replace it with joy and fulfillment, imagine what we could accomplish - or as important, imagine how good we'd feel right now. Maybe that is the biggest accomplishment James has shown us." *Terry Taylor - Creative Director*

Find out where to buy: www.NonsenseDivide.com

Pointers On My Path

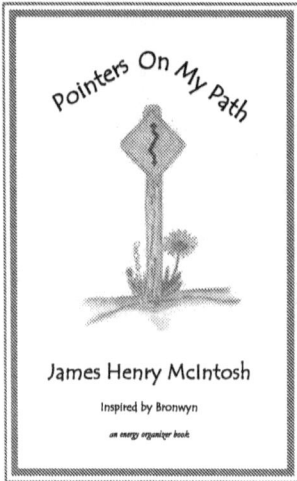

Pointers On My Path

James Henry McIntosh

Inspired by Bronwyn

an energy organiser book

Pointers on my path are these
Signs all along my way
The wood I saw beyond the trees
Thoughts that helped me not to stray

But stray I did, down cul-de-sacs
And highways smooth and broad
'Til toll roads and heavy packs
Showed wrong ways that falsely awed

With you I now would like to share
These Pointers on my Path
I know their wisdom is not rare
So read them in your bath!

"Who really wrote these poems?" This is a question I ask myself every time I read one of these poems. The first 'poem' popped out almost-complete on 18 July 1992; the last one surfaced on 22 July 1994. And that was it. Almost two years to the day and then no more.

I offer these poems to you to make of what you will. May you find the signposts amusing enough to stop you searching for 'hidden meanings'. There are none. At least, I think not.

However, you may read into them any meaning *you* wish. That is their purpose – to bring to the surface thoughts and feelings intertwined. But be on your guard, for when your thoughts and feelings come to the surface all intertwined, you too may unexpectedly start writing in rhyme with some reason.

Find out where to buy: www.NonsenseDivide.com

You've read the book.
Now listen to the CD

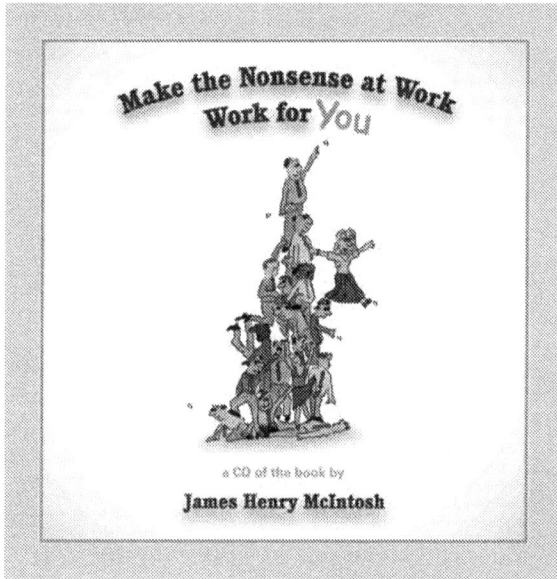

Make the Nonsense at Work Work for You

a CD of the book by

James Henry McIntosh

Find out where to buy: www.NonsenseAtWork.com

What Every Boss Needs To Know
Learning to Keeping Your Frog in Your Pocket
by Dr Wally Johnston & Linda Martin

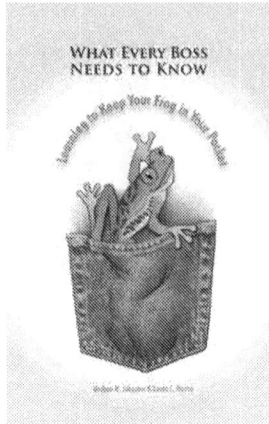

This is a simple book with some not so simple thoughts. It provides a boss or anyone who wants to be a boss to better understand and boss in the most effective way.

Using the Performance Formula, it isolates the variables that directly impact work. Dealing with the variables is the charge of a boss. By direct or indirect influence, bosses deal with the relationship between employees attributes, energy levels and their own behaviors. The result of dealing with the variables determines the level of performance and the success or failures of bosses.

The book helps the reader draw together the symbiotic nature of relationships and how to integrate them for the purpose of being an effective boss.

"A quick read... fun... great information to help you manage more effectively. Putting it simply: Just keep your Frog in your pocket and you are sure to be a winner." *Jim Wilson - President, Wilson Motivational*

Find out where to buy: www.NonsenseAtWork.com

NonsenseAtWork.com

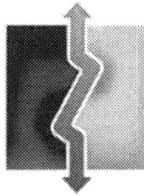

NonsenseDivide.com